Contents

What bats look like............. 2

Small bats................................ 4

Big bats..................................... 8

Bats at home...................... 10

How bats fly...................... 12

What bats catch 14

Glossary............................... 16

WHAT BATS LOOK LIKE

There are lots and lots of bats. All bats have fur on them.

Look at these bats. What do they look like?

SMALL BATS

This bat is small. It can fit into small gaps.

This bat is small. Its home is a small box.

This bat is very, very small. It can fit into a very small box.

It can fit into a very small gap. Its home is a gap in the wall.

BIG BATS

This is a very big bat. It has red fur.

It looks like a fox. It is called a flying fox.

BATS AT HOME

These bats are at home. They all live in the same home.

Bats stay at home in the day. They stay at home all day.

HOW BATS FLY

Bats have wings and can fly. They flap their wings and can fly. What do their wings look like?

Bats can fly in the dark. This bat can fly very fast.

WHAT BATS CATCH

This bat has sharp teeth. It can catch bugs with its sharp teeth.

This big bat can catch fish. It can catch fish with its sharp claws.

Glossary

claws

dark

fly

fur

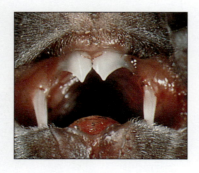
teeth

wings